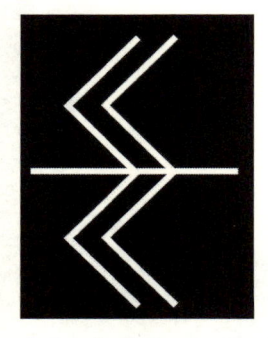

A Broken River Books original

Broken River Books
10660 SW Murdock St
#PF02
Tigard, OR 97224

Copyright © 2015 by Robert Spencer

Cover art and design copyright © 2015 by Matthew Revert
www.matthewrevert.com

Interior design by J David Osborne

All rights reserved. No part of this book may be reproduced or transmitted in any form or by any means, electronic or mechanical, including photocopying, recording, or by any information storage and retrieval system, without the written consent of the publisher, except where permitted by law.

This is a work of fiction. All names, characters, places, and incidents are the product of the author's imagination. Where the names of actual celebrities or corporate entities appear, they are used for fictional purposes and do not constitute assertions of fact. Any resemblance to real events or persons, living or dead, is coincidental.

ISBN: 978-1-940885-34-6

Printed in the USA.

The nice suit my friend loaned me was wrinkled and soiled.

EVERYTHING USED TO WORK

Donald, I love your words. I hope you enjoy

Bob Spencer

by
Robert Spencer

BROKEN RIVER BOOKS
PORTLAND, OR

Table of Contents

Gut Wiser	2
Steel Snake	3
Loose Wing Nut	4
Peckerhead Jones	5
County Line Booze Fight	7
Love at First Sight	8
Gift Horse	10
A Prayer from a Civil War Soldier	12
Tension	13
Good Morning America	15
Silt	17
Morning Glow	18
Cutting the Weeds	19
Cut It All Loose	21
Recipe for Fine Living	22
Getting It	24
Ghosts	26
Mother Nature	28
The Peeper	29
Eunuch	31
When Crab Trees Holler	32
Discovery	33
Anterior Cages	35
The Fresher the Better	36
Asshole Sun	37
400 Miles	38
Foul Ball	40
Funny Bone	41

Bean Dip	42
Around the Campfire with Bob	43
Winnie the Pooh and Tigger Too	44
The Big Squeeze	45
Coffee Stain	46
Firewater	47
Lonesome Was Usually the Way	48
Interpretive Dance	49
Chicken Shit	50
Five in the Morning	52
Piss Pants	55
How Did Hell Get In a Half Shell?	56
Turning on the Dead	57
Pussy Power	58
Naked Truth	59
Horseshoe	60
Common Swarm	62
Bat Guano	64
Cat Puke Lullaby	65
Run-Down	66
Ice Ladder	67
Out Cold	68
Sad Town	69
Respects for a Stranger	70
Rickety Dogs and Old Tricks	71
Pumice	72
Sock	73
Get It While It's Hot	75
Pancakes On Parade	76
Silted In	77
Out Of Orbit	78

Mistaken Identity	79
Since You've Been Gone	80
No Water For The Fire	81
Sore Feet	82
Another Chance	83
Broil Brain	84
Chicken Killer	85
Conundrum at the Old #9	86
Burn Pile	87
Just One More Poker Game	88
Jack-Of-All-Shades	90
Endwise Drip	92
Sentimental Stagnation	93
Skin	95
Needle in a Haystack	96
Nutritional Tip	98
R.J.	99
Catfish	100
Barry	101
Knocking 'Em Back	102
Wild Hog	103
Snipper Claw	105
Stamped in the Ass	107
Zilch	108
Puking Bobs	109
Benedictions	110
All Stopped Up	111
Paving The Way	112
Remedy	114
Leftover	115
Beer Ticket	117

Charmer	118
Low Pressure	119
Brother Angus	120
Lucky Horseshoe	121
Midway	122
Up to the Rafters	123
Drunken Dance Floor Girls	124
The Meadow is Always Slipperier on the Other Side of the Fence	125
Root Beer Fizz	126
Saving it for Later	127
Polishing The Empties	128
Sweet Breath	129
Seeing Will Squander Your Vision	130
Rain Dance	131
Laminated Heart on a Keychain	133
Obscured by Shit	134
Wintertide	135
Blood Cells and Barbed Wire	137
Where Angels Go to Hell	139
A Line in the Dirt	141
Original	143
Norman Nights	144

EVERYTHING USED TO WORK

for
John Raymond

Well-Done

Death warmed over like a boiling stew.
The cauldrons on fire
and the devil's on the loose.
Teeter on the heater,
drink a chocolate mousse.
Carve a grave at sunrise,
wave good-bye to the caboose.
Liquor is the kicker.
I'm ready to cook the goose.

Gut Wiser

It's time to put your ducks in a row
and wring their necks one by one.
When you have a curdle moustache from
drinking rotten milk, be a man
and take another drink.
It would be wise to burn your life map
and make explosives to blow potholes
in the road you've chosen.
Kick father time in his crotchety old
crotch and steal a few minutes to do
what you want without repercussions.
If you lead your horse to water
and the bastard won't drink it,
just remember he'll make a fine stew.
Shooting slingshots at glass houses
seems like about the best thing
anyone could ever do.

Steel Snake

The water is standing in the field.
All that alfalfa seed was a waste of money
and time.
The river has come in and eaten away all
the fill dirt exposing the pipeline
like a steel snake in the sun.
The oil company is as elusive
as an extinct bird.
It's going to take a lot of money to fix
the drainage in the field.
It's going to take a good crop
to make the money.
All these things weigh on a man.
It doesn't hardly seem worth it
to farm anymore.

Loose Wing Nut

Jam the pedal down, squeal the tires, and jut your
face forward with veins popping out like worms.
Stop and get your tow-sack full of pistols and shoot
every tire you see all the way down that long stretch
of highway.
Drink beer,
shift gears.
Peel the rubber clean off the Firehawks, and flip off
the moon for taking the night off way too soon.
Staying way to awake as the motor purrs through
your brain like cats wigging out after wallowing
around in catnip.
When you get bored steer your car off the road
and make your own through wheat fields.
Let it out or sweat it out.

Peckerhead Jones

Peckerhead Jones was one mean,
devil bastard right from the start.
When he was a baby his mamma
bottle-fed him lard.
As a child he had a knack
for setting fires.
He burned up the church
and the whole damn choir.
No one ever knew who did it,
but if you asked him
he'd proudly admit it.
Peckerhead Jones was a lover of knives.
First he practiced on the hogs.
Then he gutted his wives.
When the cops came snooping around
he went on the lam.
He stabbed a man named Paul
and blew the head off Paul's brother Sam.
Peckerhead Jones went on a killin' streak.
He murdered nine people
in less than a week.
A Sheriff caught up to him in New Mexico,

but ol' Peckerhead got the upper hand.
The Sheriff begged for his life,
but Peckerhead had other plans.
When they found the Sheriff he was
hanging from a cottonwood tree.
The cops raced back to town
after getting a lead.
They found Peckerhead Jones bedding
down with a whore.
He jumped out the window as
they smashed in the door.
The cops cornered him in an alley
near the edge of town.
Peckerhead took out five more
before they shot his ass down.

County Line Booze Fight

Ramshackled bum fucked fuckers squaring
off in the county line bar ditch.
They're teasers and pleasers pushing each
other down in the mud instead of taking
a swing.
Pick-ups and hot rods are parked all over
the harvested cornfield and the shitfaced
bloodthirsty crowd is cheering for them
to kill each other.
Cans of beer and cups of Everclear are
pouring down the gullets.
Several couples are vomiting and fucking
across the road in the pecan grove.
Stab it and steer.
Violence makes some people feel romantic.

Love at First Sight

People talk about love at first sight.
I don't know if I believe that.
I do believe in lust at first sight.
Two people that are instantly attracted
to each other.
Animal instincts flying off the
Richter scale.
It's one thing to fuck someone,
and quite another to find out if
you can stand that person long
enough to take it somewhere else.
Men have boners for women constantly,
everywhere they go.
Instant attraction.
Just because one woman out of all those
women happened to be attracted to you
at the same time don't mean shit.
Your parents might have told you:
"When our eyes locked it was love
at first sight."
Oh, what a magical romantic story

that is.
In truth your daddy wanted to fuck
your momma on the spot right
there on the floor.
Depending on the time period in which
your parents were born, society — and
by that I mean religion — might have
instilled in her that she is not that
kind of girl and wants to take
things slow.
She probably wanted sex too,
if it weren't for fear of infuriating
the lord.
God, apparently, don't like dicks inside
pussies unless there's a ceremony involved
that, once performed, gives permission
for penetration.
Which brings us back to love at first sight.
I believe two people can be attracted
to each other simultaneously.
And I also believe those two people
could eventually fall in love and possibly
spend their lives together.
Even the most improbable things
can happen.
But love at first sight is just a
romantic myth.
I don't believe in horseshit unless
it comes from a horse's ass.

Gift Horse

Your gift horse is gumming his oats.
He's swaybacked and club footed.
The flies swarm him as if they know
that he's rotting from the inside out.
Your gift horse won't quit eating the
pigweed and his shit looks like soup
day at school.
He's got gout and an inner ear infection
that sends a lightning bolt of pain to the
core of his brain every time a dog barks.
Your gift horse has a foul disposition
and he wishes he could kick sideways
like a mule and break your femur bone.
He hears voices in his head but he doesn't
understand English, so he follows what he
figures they are telling him to do, such as
eating, shitting, pissing, and swatting
flies with his tail.
He doesn't really like someone telling him
what to do, even though they are things
he likes to do.

If your gift horse ever looks you in the mouth,
then he is silently judging you and plotting
a way to put you out of your misery.

A Prayer from a Civil War Soldier

The green earth keeps on giving things you never
would have thought of before:
Red Bulls, tanks of tequila, and whiskey on a
mountain at dawn.
The foot of the foothills are yielding more gunpowder.
We'll be firing our mouths and muskets at noon.
Dear lord we need more whore handouts.
So please send them bitches real soon.

Tension

We sit around her apartment drinking
beer until 2:00 A.M.
then climb into bed.
Short shirt and panties,
silky legs against me.
My sex drive is at a fiery peak
after having my car towed
for driving with a suspended license.
Paying to get my car back,
paying to get my license back.
Caught in a financial hell, I needed a release.
I begin stroking her thigh and move in for the kill.
"I'm tired," she said,
and rolled to the other side of the bed.
Frustration erupts my body,
my one chance gone.
Sexual tension is boiling inside.
She falls asleep.
I slip into the bathroom, turn on the fart fan
to break the silence, and jack off.
It had been a week's worth of, "I'm not horny,"

and it had been a week's worth of bills,
the fart fan,
and my hand.
The tension is somewhat released.
Bed seems like the best thing now.
I creep back across the pitch black apartment
stumbling over empty beer bottles.
Climb under the covers,
light a cigarette,
smoke it down.
Snuff it out along with my consciousness.

Good Morning America

Moonshooter had a real hard time
waking up.
He sat slouched on
the edge of his bed.
His eyes were puffy
and his brown hair was greasy.
He stared at the floor,
all of his concentration
on the sickness in his stomach.
Used to, he would have taken
a crap and hoped for the best.
But by now, he knew that was a ruse.
On his knees, the toilet smelled
of piss and a few pubic hairs
were stuck to the bowl.
It only took one tiny toggle
of the little punching bag in his throat
before a driving force of vomit
exploded forth.
Moonshooter heaved four or five
more heaping helpings of puke

before he caught his breath.
He wiped his mouth with
a piece of toilet paper
then he wiped the splattered
mess from the toilet's mouth.
He lay back on the tile
and the sweat began
to cool on his face.

Silt

It's all in my head
Silted in like a sandbar
Time trapped in layers

Morning Glow

Basking in the orange rays at sunrise.
The smell of coffee and breakfast hang
pleasantly in the air.
Feeling of creativity deep in my marrow.
I'm going to crack the bone open, suck it dry,
and let it dribble down my chin.

Cutting the Weeds

Sometimes, you're driven to do things you don't want to do.
Things that just don't make any sense at all.
It's times like these that you question your existence.
Were you really put here to work like a dog, to be treated like one in a hot warehouse
loading heavy boxes into trucks for a measly minimum wage?
Or spread black tar on roofs in the one-hundred degree heat while someone inside the
building below is sitting in an air conditioned office jerking off to
porn and will be making more in two months than you'll be making in a year?
You have to make ends meet, someone has to do it you tell yourself, but why me?
It's a hard thing to watch someone that is half your age advancing in a company that
doesn't even know an eighth of what you know about the job.
But, you're driven along hoping if you work hard you'll be rewarded. When the payoff
never comes you become a bitter person. You've spent half your life working for a company that don't give two shits about you. They would just as well flush you down the toilet and hire new, educated

blood to fill your position. You're old and your clothes are old and the young are so fresh and new and full of vigor and ideas on how to fix the company; and, although you know their ideas are dogshit you don't get a say in the matter.

You do your job counting the days to retirement, hoping you don't get canned due to budget cuts. You realize that you're more expendable than the new hires that are younger than your own kids. The hate begins to build when these cool wizards have advanced above you or hired into a position you were next in line for. This animosity clings to you like a suit of tarnished armor and causes a chasm between you and your spouse, so that not only is your job shit but your home life is too.

Your better half leaves and gets the house. Your marriage of twenty-seven years is crushed into dust. Your heart turns to pudding and you grovel and plead, but she's done.

It's too late for apologies.

Your boss isn't very understanding of all the time you are taking off in order to stitch your life back together. He's afraid he's going to have to cut you loose. He needs people that are going to give one-thousand percent. You tell him you'll work nights and weekends, but he's done.

The severance pay might get you by for a few months. You're tired and the thought of starting over at the age of fifty-eight makes you sick.

Sometimes, you're driven to do things you don't want to do.

Things that just don't make any sense at all.

It's times like these that you question your existence.

Cut It All Loose

Coming up out of nothing.
It's what keeps things interesting,
moving and jerking like a decapitated snake.
Lose the reins to the freight train and
let it run wild into the wilderness.
Carve your name in someone else's liver
and suck on it until you're drunk.

Recipe for Fine Living

Coke and Dickel won't do. Only Dickel and Dew will do. You might not have asked me but I sure as fuck will tell you, Dickel and Coke won't do at all.
Either way you'll get fucked up.
You better suck it down either way and buck up.
If you're buzzed off the walls and all the beer is drunk, you better not turn any sort of liquor down no matter how bad it sounds, which it won't because you're already drunk. No matter where you're at, be as drunk as you damn well please.
Especially when you're at someone's house that you don't know.
When you find a rotten gallon of milk out back throw it as hard as you can against the detached garage, and watch the curdles explode then laugh and drink more of whatever they have for free.
Jump on a pool table and kick the balls across the room.
Holler, cuss, and cause a fuss just because.
If you're buzzed off everything in the house and there's nothing left but an empty box of wine, rip the deflated bladder out of the box and squeeze every drop into your hungry mouth for all it's worth.
Cigarettes are another thing entirely.
I suggest bumming them the whole time the party is going on so you'll have your own in the long run.

If someone asks you for yours, tell them it's your last one.

So, let's go over the steps I mentioned above:

Disregard Coke and Dickel because it don't make a shit's worth of nothing now.

Don't turn down liquor no matter what.

Drink as much as you want no matter where the hell you're at, most especially when you are at someone else's house that you don't know.

Throw a rotten gallon of milk against the cocksucker's house that you don't know any damn way.

Jump on a pool table and kick the balls off into space.

Ok, I have some new information for you.

A good strong sweet tea will take the bite off many a liquor.

I just mixed in three shots of vodka and I can't taste a goddamn thing.

Then again, I might be pretty drunk too.

Now back to the regular list:

Holler, cuss, and cause a fuss just because the people at the party are a fucking drag anyway.

When there's nothing left to drink, tear the bag out of a box of wine, squeeze it like the nipple of hope, and suck out every drop.

Cigarettes? Well, if you haven't figured out that game by now then you deserve to go without.

Have you learned anything fucker?

Well, maybe I haven't either.

I'm sitting here talking to you and drinking vodka mixed with sweet tea.

Getting It

The first time I remember having
an orgasm, I was about five-years-old,
almost six.
There was a tall, skinny hickory tree
that I would shimmy up and
climb onto our house.
One day, while shimmying,
I began to get a real good feeling.
The more vigorously I climbed,
the better it felt until I reached
an explosion of goodness.
I didn't know what had happened,
but I knew something very
interesting had just occurred.
After that, the urge to climb on top of
the house had a whole new meaning.
I had no conception of sex or orgasms,
but all I knew was that it felt mighty good.
I didn't tell anyone about it
and only did it when no one was around.
The good feeling I was getting

was a very private thing to me.
In my own head, I seem to remember
referring to it as "getting it."
After getting it, I would feel guilty
and a bit sad.
I was always scared I would get caught,
but I never did.
These days I have a much simpler
method of getting it.
If I can't get a woman,
I just use my trusty hand.

Ghosts

It was the sad truth during a gloomy rain.
The red dirt was sucking at the mud puddles,
and there was a calm as the drops fell on the earth.
As he stared out the window, a tsunami was erupting
in his head.
They had lived together and loved one another seventeen
years ago.
Finding out that she had just died hit him like a ton of steel.
Scars are ghosts of wounds that remind us of our sorrows.
They can eventually bleach out until our emotions for a
past lover have faded almost completely.
Out of nowhere something happens and the pain resurfaces.
The old injuries are sensitive once more.

He remembers when they first rented the house together.
Everything was exciting and new.
It lasted a little over a year, but it was the closest he'd come
to a marriage at that point.
Emotionally it was just as tasking as a divorce when it all
fell apart.
For him anyway.
One day he came home and found the Yellow Pages opened

to apartments.

Sitting alone at the kitchen table with a cinder block in his chest, he knew things were getting ready to end.

It was a long haul getting over it too.

Although he knew it was probably for the best, it was the cheating and betrayal before she revealed her intentions that gnawed at his guts.

When you are lonesome and depressed over a failed relationship, the tendency is to remember the good times.

After she moved out he felt like he could forgive her if only he could get that feeling of love back.

Like it was in the beginning.

But he knew once women were done they were usually finished.

Women are more emotional during the relationship, and men are more emotional when it's unraveling.

You never know how bad a relationship truly was until you find somebody much better.

He had.

The rain was beginning to fall a little harder outside, and he took a deep breath.

In honor of her life he felt like he should remember the good things about her.

She could command a room of guests and have them rolling with laughter.

She was a fun person to be around and a master storyteller.

Her husband and three small children were going through a hell he could not imagine.

He had not seen her or talked to her in seventeen years.

The wounds opened up and they bled.

Mother Nature

Mother Nature's got a broken nose.
A do-rag head wrap
and the hurricane jones.
Turtle shell tile for her kitchen floor.
Multiple animals in her sand stone oven
for breakfast in the morning.
She's got a red oak for a table
and fossilized bones fashioned into chairs.
Deer skin curtains and briers everywhere.
She's got an elephant skull cooking pot
for making savory stews
and gutted rabbit carcasses drying in the sun.
A ragged bear skin coat to guard
against the chill she's created tonight.
Green mossy hair with hickory stick curlers
rolled in tight.
She's got a porcupine brush
and hair spray made from lard.
Pickled eagle eyeballs stored away in jars.
She's got a massive fireplace
burning up twenty trees a day.
That lovely Mother Nature,
she is quite a lady.

The Peeper

He's a slippery little fucker way up there in the pines.
He goes out late at night with a peep show on his mind.
He likes to look in windows and watch the ladies undress.
He never does discriminate,
but it's the fat ones he likes best.
One of his regulars is a 400-pound widow named Cindy,
and he likes to watch her folds come down.
He pulls out his one-eyed weasel there in the bushes
and really goes to town.
His appetite is a bottomless hole from whence
no amount of naked women can fill.
It's the times that he almost gets caught
that really gives him a thrill.
He makes his rounds if there's snow and ice
or even if it's raining.
It was on one dark and stormy night that he saw
Tom Blanchard's wife in the bathtub shaving.
He quit visiting the Sesby twins,
he never could tell one from the other.
It weirded him out one night when he watched
them both get fucked by their brother.
You know he's out there,
peeping and carrying on.

He's already looked inside your window.
If you look close you can see his footprints
in the dew on your lawn.

Eunuch

He's a calibrated eunuch and they hit his
reset button once a week.
He lies around with hot young naked girls
and never so much as gives their rosebud
nipples a tweak.
They try to tempt him by pinning him down
and rubbing their candy clits on his face.
But he's not aroused by the sweet honey taste.
He waits and watches until a predator slips
in for some precious lamb pie.
Then he bashes in their skulls and makes
necklaces and charm bracelets out of
their eyes.
The girls wear the jewelry, laugh, dance,
and make love.

When Crab Trees Holler

Do not step out of this area.
Hold onto the wing and suck
air through your teeth.
Wrap your foot around
your brain ten times and
spray a liberal amount of
anti-fungal all over the
whole damn mess.

Discovery

It was discovered by a 4x4, tearing through
a field in the snow.
The driver thought it was a log.
A young boy named Joe watched in awe
as the 4x4 sped away.
He thought about how jealous his school friends
would be if he drove up on the playground in a 4x4.
Joe hadn't been following the tire trail long when he saw
the blood on the path.
He dug the snow from out around a dead woman.
Joe had never seen a naked woman before,
much less a naked dead woman in the snow.
She had a small bullet hole in her chest.
Her stomach a road bump.
The eyes glared into nothing.
He looked between her legs.
She didn't have what he had.
Just a tuft of hair.
He also looked at the humps on her chest.
Joe's pecker got hard, like when he stared at
Rebecca in class.
He touched the nipples on the humps.

They felt like dull icicle tips.
He reached down and touched the hair,
it was as stiff as a wire brush.
Joe covered the corpse with snow
and ran to get his buddies.

Anterior Cages

It's all carnage of the mind.
Butchered and massacred,
overrun with too many thoughts,
too many plans,
too many promises that seem to be going
somewhere — but nowhere — except a grave
already piled high with bloated corpses.
The memories are filled with tormented thoughts
of gnarled roots:
twisting and turning,
writhing and growing, trying to tear its way
into the stinging air.
Bringing insanity to the forefront.
Leaving dark silence in a piss-ridden corner,
drooling and muttering about the repetitive past.
They're both in there:
past and present scrapping it out over
the here and now, the what's already been.
Both holding their own.
While the world turns, changes,
and moves on for good or ill.

The Fresher the Better

It's all fresh here every day!
It's all fresh here every day!
Bill's digital watch beeps every hour.
Only two lousy beeps so far this morning.
Another day that creeps by like frozen
molasses.
Yet another shitpile job steaming in the sun.
It's all fresh here every day!
It's all fresh here every day!
Throw your heap of crap up on the
scale and save.

Asshole Sun

Shafted by the middle finger sun.
The humidity is drawing saltwater
from every pore like a lonely
sponge beached in the hot sand.

400 Miles

By time I found the one, I had been living
in an apartment in Oklahoma City three years,
with very few women to account for
during that time.
There was one short-lived love affair with a good
friend of mine that had already moved
400 miles away.
She had come to visit for a wedding,
a mutual friend of ours.
I offered to let her stay at my place
and she did.
We ended up alone there, drinking and
laughing, and one thing lead to another.
She was on her period, but I couldn't give
two shits less.
I threw a towel down on the bed,
and we made love.
The weekend immediately became magical.
It ended like all things must, and she went
back home 400 miles away.
We wrote letters by mail and talked

occasionally on the phone.
I sat alone in my apartment drinking too much
and pining for her.
A trip was planned and I flew to see her
for the weekend, but the magic
was seemingly gone.
We went to parties and clubs, but she
was unwilling to have sex.
At one of the parties I got rowdy and broke
some shit, and she wouldn't let it go.
The next morning she was in a bad mood,
and she bitched at me for my behavior
the night before.
I was hungover as hell, bedraggled,
and a bit ashamed.
The things that annoyed me
about her flooded back.
The fact that when she read my stuff,
she would say:
"That's shock value. All you write is shock."

I flew back with my dick tucked
between my legs.
When I got to my apartment,
I made love to the walls,
the floor,
the ceiling,
and the flies that buzzed
around the empty beer cans.

Foul Ball

He wished he was a killer on the run.
He would have a hot female sidekick that he'd fuck along their murder spree.
Not only could he never kill anybody — though he had many fantasies — he couldn't get a girlfriend to save his life.
It's been over a year since he's been laid.
It wasn't for lack of trying.
He earned and wore the tarnished jeweled crown of The Strikeout King.
It felt like thorns digging into the hard-on in his brain.

Funny Bone

He drags his ass through a sticker patch.
Grits his teeth and sucks it up.
He flutters his arms like chicken wings
and sounds off like a peacock.
A cocklebur drives its spikes right into
his anus.
He clinches his buttocks around the barbs
and laughs.
It's his ticklish spot.

Bean Dip

The first time I tried bean dip I was five.
A kid I barely knew shared some corn chips
and bean dip with me at a church picnic.
I was surprised at how well I liked it.
We both talked about how good bean dip was
and that's the only conversation I remember having with him.
I saw him around on the school playground,
and occasionally at church, but we never hung out again.
Two years later his mother stabbed him thirty-seven times
with a butcher knife.
She claimed he was chock-full of demons.

Around the Campfire with Bob

Beer can walking a burning plank.
Sad eyes crying in the blaze,
crossing over into nowhere.
A land with a smoke-stained kiss.
Ember cunt disintegrates the cock,
and the dickless asshole runs howling
through the woods.
Jesus told me to kill the rat in the cellar
with a double-bladed wood cutting axe
with a laser scope.
Chewing on raw cement.
Pigging out on chicken livers.
Workin' for a fire is tiresome work.
Got the Angel of Death in a half-nelson.
This fire is a slave drivin' motherfucker.
Armadillo on the half-shell.
Gotta hole in my house.
Grandma got sick.
Dog got sick.

Winnie the Pooh and Tigger Too

I would stare at Winnie the Pooh
and Tigger too
when I fucked her from behind.
They were inked in bright colors
just above the ass.
Tigger had pounced on top of Pooh's belly,
looking happily down at Pooh.
Pooh was confused.

Sometimes I would think
back to when I was a little boy.
I liked watching Winnie the Pooh.
I was a bit confused by Tigger myself.

I would stare at Winnie the Pooh
and Tigger too hanging out
just above her ass while I thrusted away.
I didn't feel like a little boy.

The Big Squeeze

Dog with its eyeball hanging out.
Bald headed woman short and stout.
She's got thighs of iron,
and when you're locked in
she'll show you what it's all about.
Snapping pussy clamped down
like a vice.
Once you're inside
you won't think twice.
She works you over until you pop.
Grinds and grinds until you scream,
"Stop!"
When she's done you're on the floor.
She struts away
like a victor of war.

Coffee Stain

Blood moon seeping out of the pillowcase.
Translucent shadows gauging her lonely face.
The pillow is wrung out again and again.
Lateral lines are bleeding, the tree roots
are sopping them up, and the acorns are
weeping red.
We tempt each other and stuff our coat
pockets full of berries and nuts.

Firewater

I climbed into a really hot bath to
loosen up my constipated guts.
My body screamed for a few seconds
but it got used to it.
I was submerged up to my neck,
letting the heat soak in.
While I lay there I noticed a mammoth
mosquito flying around about where
my head would be if I were
taking a shower.
It began descending towards my head.
When it got to eye level it shot back up.
Mosquitoes are smarter than I thought.
My blood was still poisoned by whiskey
and beer from the night before.
Mosquitoes already fly in doddering circles.
I can't imagine how dumb
a drunk mosquito would look.

Lonesome Was Usually the Way

Laughing arms when there's nothing else to do.
Loving lips angled with mine.
All locked in and ready for the ride.
Wild euphoria out in the woods.
The moon is nibbling and I am too.

Interpretive Dance

Armadillos smoking crack and doing an underwater dance.
They can cut a rug up to ten minutes or so.
Then they climb to the surface for a mighty fine blow.

Chicken Shit

We were in New Orleans at a club during Mardi Gras
after eight hours of drinking and two hits of acid.
My face was painted red, and I was wearing a
multi-colored suit jacket that I had bought at a thrift store.
Girls were getting on stage, lifting their shirts,
and showing their tits.
I was screaming and hollering and leaning over the rail
with a big cigar in my mouth.
A big bruiser of a bouncer, who apparently thought I was
having too much fun, came over and told me to leave.
He escorted me to the exit door.
I could see my friends inside, looking at me and laughing.
I held up my finger in a one-minute gesture.
I went to the entrance door, showed them my stamped
hand, got a beer, and rejoined my friends.
A few minutes later after I was yelling at the girls on
stage, the bouncer spotted me again.
"I thought I told you to get the fuck
out of here."
"Ok, ok, I'm not goddamn hurting anybody."
"I don't give a shit."

Once again I was escorted to the exit, and once more I gestured at my friends with the one-minute finger.
I showed my stamp at the door, and as I walked to the bar I was ambushed by the bouncer.
"You fucking son of a bitch!"
He grabbed my arm and shoved me all the way to the exit. Grabbing my ponytail, he swung me out on the sidewalk into a group of black guys.
"What the fuck was that for?" one guy asked me.
"That sorry cocksucker thinks I'm having
too much fun." I pointed at the bouncer who
stood angrily in the exit with his arms folded.
Then they all started cussing him:
"You're just a goddamn chicken shit."
"Won't you pick on someone your own size
you stupid motherfucker?"
"You're just a big ol' lump of shit."
He looked pissed as we continued insulting him until he finally walked away.
He could have taken my drunken ass, but he wasn't going to try to take on the mob that had come to my aid.
My friends came out.
It was the third bar we had been kicked out of that day.
We walked to the bar next door, and I ordered a beer.

Five in the Morning

By 5:00 A.M. in New Orleans during Mardi Gras,
I was completely blown out of my gourd.
My friend told me later that we were standing
in line at a fast food joint on Bourbon Street
when I handed some random guy in line with us
a dollar bill and walked out the door.
I ended up on a dark deserted street with
my teeth chattering from the chill.
I was wearing a multi-colored suit jacket
and my face was painted red.
A nice silver Lexus pulled up
and the passenger window came down.
A black woman was driving
and she leaned over and said:
"You look like you need a ride."
The car looked nice and warm.
I opened the door and got inside.
We drove along a little ways and
she asked: "Have you ever been with
a black woman before?"
"No I haven't."

"Oh lord honey, you don't know
what you been missin'."
It sounded like I had been missing
out on a lot.
"You got any money?"
"Some."
"How much?"
I pulled out my wallet but I
was too fucked up to count.
"Boy, you sure are a sight. Let me see that."
She took the billfold, counted the bills,
and handed it back.
We pulled into a turn around by
the lobby of a nice hotel.
"Ok honey, meet me outside of room 302.
I'm going to park the car, and then we'll
have us a good time."
"Alright."
I walked into the lobby and the guy
at the counter looked at me funny.
In fact, everyone I passed as I walked
down the hall with the room numbers
looked at me weird.
As fucked up as I was,
I began to get suspicious.
What if she meets me at the room,
lets me in, and some big motherfucker
beats my ass?
I didn't try to find the room.
I sat down on a bench instead.
When I woke up and walked back to the lobby

the sun was out.
There were two good-looking girls
at the counter.
I stopped and looked at them and they
had the strangest expressions on their faces.
I went out the door and started
down the sidewalk.
I turned a corner and went along aimlessly,
without a care in the world.
I had no worries on how I was going
to find our hotel, or my friends.
I was heading toward the Mississippi River
in the warm sun.
I had been walking for maybe five minutes
when my friend's CRX came zipping up
beside me.
He hopped out and said:
"My god, where have you been?
I can't believe we found you!"
"We've been driving around for hours
looking for you when we spotted that
goddamn jacket. You're three fucking
miles away from Bourbon Street!"
I got in the car, and we headed off
to the London Inn.

Piss Pants

I woke up in the hotel room
wearing piss pants, and I didn't care.
The nice suit my friend loaned me
was wrinkled and soiled.
Got up and looked in the Margarita bucket.
It was a quarter of the way full.
Margarita went down smooth and refreshing.
I stopped at a corner store to buy cigarettes.
The clerk pointed out
a three pack for the price of two.
I took the deal.
On the way to my car, a bum walked up.
"Hey buddy, could I get a cigarette from you?" he asked.
"Sure," I said. "Here, have a pack."
"Thanks man," he said. "It'll come back to you."
I figured it would.
We shook hands.
He headed off into a field behind the store.
I felt good.
The sun was out.
I was wearing piss pants and I didn't care.

How Did Hell Get In a Half Shell?

When's a killer truly a killer?
What makes a kite burst into flames
and nosedive into a dead tree?
Why do bees kiss you on the stomach until
honey drips out of your bellybutton?
Can't a mosquito drive a finishing nail
through the foreskin of an elephant?
Isn't it logical that a rat's tongue be used
to scour the dirty pans in the sink?
These are questions commonly asked
in the grand scheme of life.
If we all pull together we can make it
happen y'all.

Turning on the Dead

It keeps my pecker hard
listening to you talk in the graveyard
while eating sliced cantaloupe and peaches
from your grandfather's farm.
I'm leaning against
WALTER HEMLEY'S tombstone:
1870 to 1910.
You're lying where I can almost see up your dress.
A gentle thigh rising
then sloping towards truth.
The hem of your dress just blocks your delight.
A fingernail moon is visible through the trees.
You rise up suddenly, and move in close to me.
Hard as a hog's leg, but not as long.
I pull your dress to the side, and your panties are the sun.
Yanking them off, I enter heaven's gate.
I don't last very long before I fill you up inside.
Seeing you smile, everything is all right.

Pussy Power

The power of pussy can reduce men to blubber.
It can eat through steel doors and reduce mountains
to anthills.
The power of pussy is beautiful and hideous
and sits upon a throne in the most grotesque of shrines.
The pussy is the most elegant of clams, and has the
most exquisite pearls inside.

Naked Truth

His face was sallow and so was his soul.
He had mixed feeling in a fruit punch bowl.
The bottom of his feet was so tough a nail
couldn't penetrate them.
Went barefoot in the machine shop he worked
at while singing gospel hymns.
Didn't allow any cussing or taking the lord's
name in vain.
Had a strict rule against drinking:
better not catch you with no whiskey stains.

Horseshoe

Given unto things we don't know.
Letting our fears grow like greasy tumors.
Blind eyes staring through shades of purple and grey.
Disowning, disarming, dismembering the conductivity
of a flat dull world.
An empty cavity filled with rotting bodies that are
trying their damnedest to come back to life.
Like ants we wage war.
The only difference is that ants have better reasons
than we do.
Totem poles buried up to their necks in dust,
pondering bygone days when things were a
little newer, a little fresher — when they themselves
were younger and dumber like the rest of us.
Starving like rabid cusses around a table of gold.
Trampling the downtrodden with the bootheels of
our soul.
Salt water sea chaffing your ass, but your sore asshole
still gleams like a ruby in the mid-afternoon sun.
Skipping stones across a river made from human piss.
Now the stone has T.B., Chlamydia, herpes,

and the syph.
A plane tailspins into the roof of your daddy's car.
Your skin is full of shattered bone, if someone shakes you it sounds like a maraca.
I don't know what to do with myself.
I'm as listless as a dog after a fox hunt.
Falling down a flight of stairs.
Get up and shake off the fleas.
Don't give me all that shit about how you're as busy as a bee.
Time cascades across dirty sheets of ice.
Throw out the bags of salt and try to slow that bastard down.
He always seems to find a way to catch back up.
Grasshoppers eating the farmer's crops.
Their greedy mouths chewing on their cud.
For all they know it was grown just for them.
Who could blame them?
The drought affects them too.
Wish in one hand and piss in the other.
Urine might be nice and warm but it'll fall through your fingers and evaporate.
Zero equals zero.
Back to square one.

Common Swarm

Their voices rose and blended together
like a swarm of insects.
    Faces:
old gentle faces,
old gnarled oak tree faces,
young parent faces.
Frosted, housewife perms.
Short, nondescript workingman haircuts.
Children in highchairs.
Children big enough to sit in a chair.
Words appear here and there
out of the droning noise.
They are swallowed up
by other audible clichés.
Everyone is shoveling food into their mouths.
Silverware is clanking like a blacksmith shop.
I step outside.
The air is cold.
It feels good breathing it in and out.
The only sounds:
the wind blowing,

my car starting,
me tearing hell out of there.
Leaving the insects behind.

Bat Guano

The bats have risen and have gone.
Their dung is smeared all over the lawn.
My wife slipped on the guano and busted open her head.
She threw her clothes in the washer, stepped in the
shower, and fell face first into the floral tile dead.
A freak of nature:
the bats eliminated the one I wanted to destroy.
She was a good fuck, but she constantly nagged and
annoyed.
I had planned on poisoning her at our anniversary dinner
that very night.
Of course, that was before those incredible bats swooped
in, and took her out with their foul-smelling slippery shit.

Cat Puke Lullaby

Going to bed late and finding nasty
wet cat vomit all over the sheets
can really bring a man down.
All you can do is change them,
go to sleep, and hope to dream
of better things.

Run-Down

Time cascades across a sheet of ice.
Weary wanderers wondering where it all went.
Sapphires always shine brightest
before dawn.
It's been a haggard journey just for it all to
come down to mowing this stupid lawn.
All that was has decomposed into the past.
When the last breath is taken all the memories
will be lost like freeze dried specks of sand.

Ice Ladder

I don't feel like the smartest person in the world
climbing up a ladder completely encased in ice,
in my house shoes, to spray de-icer on
the satellite dish.
But I did do that, and I was in my pajamas with
no coat on to boot.
So, I guess there's not much to be said, other
than I felt secure enough on the ice ladder.
To support this I accomplished my goal without
incident or injury.
In fact, I climbed up the ice steps at least three
times, so I think I know what I'm doing,
so fuck you!

Out Cold

He lay on the ground, flat on his back,
where he had fallen off the tailgate
of the pick-up.
He wasn't breathing, and his eyes were
rolled partially into his head.
Me and Two Thumb Poo Jack hovered
over him yelling his name:
"Dad, dad."
"Jerry, Jerry."
"He's out cold," Two Thumb Poo Jack said.
He didn't look like he was breathing,
and I gave my father mouth to mouth
without hesitation.
Immediately, he started
coming around.
Looking straight into my face
with glazed eyes,
he feebly reached for me.

Sad Town

Guaranteed sadness for a buck.
It's a deal that's hard to refuse.
Whatever gauge of melancholy you want.
It's all the same price:
from just a case of the mopes,
to a suicidal delirium and everything
in-between, it's one dollar.
If you want to sidle into your
abysmal depression then we suggest the
eight dollar deal,
which allows you eight subtle levels before
you off yourself.
Then there's always the kind of people
that just want to get down to it.
They want to save the seven bucks and
stampede straight into the noose.
So, if you want to cry for an hour or a few
days, or just have a general case of the blues,
call and make an appointment at: 1-800-SADTOWN…
that's 1-800-SADTOWN.
We'll have plenty of tissue for you.

Respects for a Stranger

The funeral procession rolls into the cemetery.
My yellow beast is screaming at the top of its lungs next door.
Sour earth upturned,
paddles flipping dirt skyward.
I shut my beast down in respect.
I watch them carry the casket to the grave.
Old people, young people, people carrying children.
The service begins.
Heads hung,
handkerchiefs raised.
Handsome suits and pretty dresses.
I watch as the cars slowly begin to leave.
They seem slow and languid as they go by.
Grim faces reflecting on the past.
The empty shell they're leaving behind used to
breathe and drive away from cemeteries,
grieving her loved ones.

Rickety Dogs and Old Tricks

Trampling the dead back out of their graves.
Teaching them how to dance all over again.
They're slow learners the second time around.
They like suckers a lot and coloring quite a bit.
Their color scheme is way out of whack.

Pumice

Sitting around on a graveyard stump
The plots gonna thicken
like fryin' up chitlins
Catching flies and raisin' chickens
Everyone's getting tired of your bitchin'
Alimony acrobat cracking the whip
Newsstand photographs of a sunken ship
Cram your mouth with ceremony
Scrub your balls with a sandy secret

Sock

My friend's mother, newly separated
from his father, frequently
brought men home to fuck.
She was a heavy, unattractive bleach blonde
with big thick lips that she kept painted
with bright red lipstick.
Their back porch was screened in,
and she had a full sized mattress thrown
down there on the concrete that she would
take naps on, even sleep on at night
when the weather was nice.
One of the men she was fucking for a few weeks
was a husky, bearded loudmouth
named Stewart.
My friend and I were thirteen.
We were riding in the back seat,
Stewart was driving and the
mother riding shotgun.
Stewart talked loudly about how they
didn't have any rubbers the night before
and had to use a sock.

The mother shot him a dirty look,
and with a stupid grin on his face he said,
"What? What?"
Stewart was just one of the many dumb-shits
my friend's mother dragged home.

Get It While It's Hot

Quit trying to make something positive
out of horseshit.
Some things are just as crappy as they seem.
Not everything has a hidden meaning below
the surface of a turd.
You don't always have to smell it and taste
it to figure out that it's shit.
A lot of things are just what they appear to be...
a piping hot fresh pile of dung.

Pancakes On Parade

Crippled up from fanfare
of the illicit kind.
Tempered by allegories that
flatulate like a Christmas bomb
in a meat market.
Upwards, endwise, and dropped
to belly bust on the pavement.
Stagnant eyes fishing for a
better view.
Looking for gossip while chewing
on chicken fat.
Absurdities are willing to fight
back with a vengeance.
Stupidity, as always, is holding
up its part of the deal.

Silted In

mindless transfers
hernia churns
sun baked alabaster
fuck that cunt just a little bit faster
up on the high side
low on the down
haven't got that much to hide
gotta choke down that cocklebur pride
aging landfills
buried bodies waiting to be killed
constant aggravation
townhouse masturbation
letter she wrote said:
   you're a dolt
I'm gonna catch a ride on the mystery boat
hope those corpses don't stay afloat
my eyeball has gone to root
guess the other will follow suit
the loamy soil really makes
those bad boys go to town

Out Of Orbit

There are billions of worlds on one planet.
If you shit on mine I'll run my lateral
lines through the center of yours.
If you fuck with mine, I'll fuckin' kick
yours clean out of orbit.
There are billions of worlds on one
planet — I wrap my world in razor wire
and soak it down with a hard driving
whiskey rain.
If you don't like my world, I'll probably
hate the hell out of yours.

Mistaken Identity

"You're going to have to pull over baby," I said.
She pulled the car off the highway and drove
to an isolated spot behind a gas station.
Getting out, I hunkered down by the back tire
and vomit spewed out of my mouth.
The tequila hadn't sat well on top of
the Budweiser and apricot chicken.
I saw an SUV drive up beside our car
and stop for a second.
Well hidden from view,
I was ramming my finger down my throat
trying to empty all the shit out of my guts.
I finished and got inside the car.
"That guy propositioned me for a blowjob," she said.
She showed me how he gestured with his hand,
like a cock going in and out of his mouth.
"He thought you were a dirty little whore," I said laughing.
She laughed too.
Pulling over one more time on our way home
I couldn't get much to come out.
We drove on in, me and my beautiful girl,
who was mistaken for a hooker.

Since You've Been Gone

You've been gone quite a few years now,
but I still think about you.
I've become good friends with your son,
and although I'm not the best role model,
I'm not all bad either.
I hang out with him and make sure he's
doing alright.
Your death has been extremely hard on him
like it would be for any teenager.
He's never really talked to me about it much
and I've never pressured him to.
I've told him funny things you've said
and, from time to time, he has asked me to
retell them.
As I sat and watched his high school
graduation, I thought about how damn
proud you would be.
He's turned into a fine human being.
I see a lot of you in him.
It's like you're still around.

No Water For The Fire

It was a breezeway into a hornet's nest sun.
I kept coming toward them and they stung
the shit out of my eyes and my soul.
I swung my arms and kept on going.

Sore Feet

Smorgasbord of never ending obstacles
Airplane crashed before I could board
Plans took a nosedive into a rocky shore
My instincts take me down a maze
of gnarled roots
Shards of light pierce the darkness
I lick the light and beg for the sun

Another Chance

Crusted saliva sits on the corners of the mouth
like aged rot.
The body huddles in the cell awaiting release.
Tarnished manipulation ringing
like polished steel.
Another chance to grip the knife.
To see eyes looking into his as life
is consumed by darkness.
Driveling lips quiver with anticipation.
An adrenaline chill sweeps through him
like an erotic lust.
The ears perk to hard soles clicking
on pavement.
His head rises to see the key unlock the door.

Broil Brain

Ripped the crotch out of my britches.
My fading smile needs hemorrhoid stitches.
Picking and blowing out dirt boogers.
Dreaming of an ice crown that I can wear
and strutting around like royalty in the 107
degree heat.

Chicken Killer

He popped a bobcat with a two-barrel shotgun.
He pulled both triggers and there wasn't much left but a rug.
"Crazy thing bin gettin' into my chickens," he grinned.
We walked back across the yard with the temperature dropping
and the sun setting in the west.
His wife made pork chops.
They were the best I ever had.
We smoked, drank coffee, and talked about bobcats.

Conundrum at the Old #9

"You can date a customer as long as he's not a stupid idiot," she said. "But how the hell you gonna find out if he's a stupid idiot if you don't date 'em?"
Then she finished her beer, got off the barstool, and went behind the bar to relieve Helen the bartender and start her own shift here at the Old #9.

Burn Pile

Gloom and doom.
Blackjack shavings in my blood.
Bruises on my legs and scrapes on my arms.
Those scraggly bastards stick together.
They fight all the way to the burning pit.
The crackle and pop in the flames
is like sweet music to my ears.
I take a slug of beer and go back for more.
Chainsaw screaming,
loppers loppin'.
Blackjacks don't care about quality,
only quantity.
They are vermin oak trees uselessly spreading
their rodent asses through the forest.

Just One More Poker Game

He cleaned the tip of the knife while drinking a beer.
He cleaned the tip of his knife,
blazed up a cigarette,
inhaled deep.
He cleaned the tip of the knife,
drank the beer,
smoked the cigarette,
and watched *My Three Sons* on the T.V.
The blade of the knife was crisp and clean
like the chime of a tuning fork.
He continued on the tip.
He turned from the T.V.
His wife was lying in a pool of blood
on the kitchen floor.
Morton was not one to take insults lightly.
Uncle Charley made a wisecrack on
the television set.
Harmonious laughter ensued.
The rest of the house was still

like when his wife was away
visiting her mother in Vermont.
Clay, Mike, and Vince would be over
pretty soon for poker.
Morton wished they could have one
last poker game to win back his loss
from last week.
He wished he could take back what he did
just so the poker game could go on.
He'd forgotten about the fucking poker game.

Jack-Of-All-Shades

Exuberant viper always on the prowl.
Slipping in and out of cracks and
straight into your inner ear.
It likes to wrap itself around
your brain and hug it.
Ever so gently sink its fangs into
your cerebral cortex and suck
out your conscious thought.
It makes you feel listless and numb.
You sleep all day and stare
at the wall a lot.
The snake likes your head:
    snuggle
      snuggle
        cuddle
          cuddle
He feels good and he's warm.
Writes profound poetry and creates
masterpieces with oil paints.
Solves mathematical equations that
have never been dreamt of before.

Snake moonlights solving
world hunger.
Drool trickles down your chin
and a small river runs down your
front and fills up your navel.
The blank wall is right where
you put it.
The snake stretches, yawns
and takes a nap.
When he wakes up he'll get
cracking on the energy crisis.

Endwise Drip

He hollered and she yodeled back.
They had a beautiful time fucking dog style on the rotunda.
Their knees stung like Indian burns, and her nose kept running like a spigot because of the goddamn
cedar pollen.
All the snot was a turn off, but looking at her tits and puss kept him hard.
Slipping it in while she wasn't facing him was the best way to execute it.
They were sitting on the floor smoking cigarettes, and she was blowing a nonstop flow of snot into her panties.
"My allergies are going fucking crazy," she said nasally.
He took the last drag of his cigarette and flicked it.
Turning her around on her hands and knees he put it in, but she kept sucking snot and after awhile he couldn't continue.
"Did I do something wrong?"
"No, I guess I'm just getting tired," he lied.
There are some things doggy style can only mask for so long, he thought.

Sentimental Stagnation

No more sentimental bullshit.
No more pocket fluff for the brain.
You say you want the dark stuff,
disasters that hit you like a train.
Things that make you feel better
to see someone else in pain.

Burning synapses,
memory cancers,
and rage.
Lifetime setbacks.
I knew I shouldn't have come this way.
Squirming through charred chambers
in a hornet's nest.
A pale sightless larva,
the air burns my skin.
Only the ones searching the dark side
of the mind dare to come within.
Society is on the surface.
I don't quite fit in.
There's too much pretentious ignorance

to hide yourself from sin.
The water's cold and murky.
I've bathed my sorrows and fears.
The water once ran pure and sacred.
Now no one ventures near.

Skin

Give me truth on laden highways
   where the tears have been.
      Shed your skin.
Carnival acts in a filthy cunt's sewer,
   the liars end.
      Shed your skin.
Sacrifice the past on an altar to the present
   dripping blood and sin.
      Shed your skin.
Fear in a line of midnight fury,
   a sorrowful elm that bends.
      Shed your skin.
Crimson tides crash belligerence,
   the mind's eye within.
      Shed your skin.
Topple the empty tables that taunt your
swollen bellies,
   that plastic could never send.
      Shed everything for me.

Needle In a Haystack

Where is it?
  Where's the goddamn aspirin?
On a binge again.
Where is it?
  Where's the fuckin' Alka-Seltzer?
On a binge again.
Where is it?
  Where's these strangers' toilet so I can puke?
On a binge again.
Where is it?
  Where's the shit suckin' light switch
  so I can peel myself off the floor?
On a binge again.
Where is it?
  Where's my car so I can drive
  my drunken ass home?
On a binge again.
Where is it?
  Where's the center line so I can
  keep myself straight?
On a binge again.

  Where is it?
   Where's my stinkin' key so I can
   get inside the door?
On a binge again.
 Where is it?
  Where's my bed?
If I've made it this far,
I won't have a problem finding
my goddamn bed.

Nutritional Tip

Goat meat is good for the soul.
Chew it up good
and all will be well.
Stomp your hooves
and bleat at the sun.

R.J.

R.J. is old.
He has blue eyes that have seen many things in his day.
We ate breakfast with him and his wife on the ship.
His wife means well, but she nags
and corrects him constantly.
R.J.'s eyes are starting to fade, but they flicker
in the company of young pretty girls.
We saw R.J. and his wife again in Mexico.
  "R.J., stop," his wife nagged.
  "R.J., stop!" she pleaded.
He was a little ways ahead.
R.J. didn't stop.
He didn't even turn around.
She chased after him and I silently cheered him on.

Catfish

Catfish likes to fish but he can't eat 'em
because he's highly allergic.
He makes a special point to tell everybody
this 4, 5, or 6 times.
He's a fat, overall wearing pain in the ass.
He likes to talk a lot about nothing.

Barry

He put the head in a brown paper grocery sack.
Rolled the top up neatly like a lunch bag
and wrote "Barry" on the side so there would be
no doubt of ownership.

Knocking 'Em Back

The beer went down in a dizzy daze.
Happy hour had been gone eight hours, but the nonsensical loud voice-raising rants and laughter were still bursting at the beer tabs.
The mouths are funnels, cans are drained, cigarettes smoked to the quick.
The orange glow on the horizon looms sickeningly: a reminder that reality is right around the corner.
The last day of freedom is spent in a state of miserable recovery.
A small consequence for a great night drinking with friends.

Wild Hog

Run through the night.
Run through the day.
Embryonic fluids pour
down like rain.
Shovel the shit.
Throw a pig on the spit.
Dance with a gal in
a galvanized pit.
Send for the guns,
the whores,
and hecklers.
Lay them out easy
in the greasy grass.
Dip out another bowl
of that sassafras.
It takes one bottle of
whiskey to make em'
look good.
He fucked fat Nellie
on the car of his hood.
Everyone's drinkin' and

chomping down on swine.
If the law interferes they'll
cut 'em down on a dime.

Snipper Claw

After Cliff Spriggs got his arm mashed off with the bucket of a front-end loader he didn't give too much of a shit about nothin'.
It happened while him and his Mexican hired hands were making repairs.
It took the Mexicans damn near five minutes to get the bucket off his ruined arm.
When the doctor cut what was left of his arm off, he had to wear a sock thing on his nub that compressed it to get it ready for a prosthetic.
All he knew was that he wanted a razor sharp snipper claw for a hand.
Maybe then people would quit asking him:
"What happened to your arm, Cliff?"
What he wanted to say was:
"What does it look like? It got mashed the fuck off, you ignorant fucking cunt!"
He imagined somebody asking:
"What happened to your arm?" and before the cocksucker had a chance to so much as bat an eye, he would snip a couple of their fingers off.

If he got a good snipper claw he would probably practice on hotdogs first.

He would make a man out of his old clothes and give him hotdog fingers.

He would become so lightning fast that the person that asked the ignorant fucking question would be waiting for an answer for a few seconds before they noticed their fingers lying on the ground.

If he had a razor sharp snipper claw he thought, everything might be all right.

It would definitely make things better.

Stamped in the Ass

Glory hole
Shot of Old Crow
Ten High bourbon sweating
out the pores
Cutting a rug with them
good time girls

Zilch

Landlocked with my head pinched in.
No way out.
Nothing left to begin.

Puking Bobs

Bob and Bob were at a party.
Bob and Bob drank a lot of whiskey.
Bob and Bob talked shit to each other
about which one was the better wrestler.
They scrapped it out on the living room floor.
Bob had Bob in a headlock.
Bob had Bob's leg locked in.
Bob was surprised at how stout Bob was,
and Bob was surprised at how stout Bob was.
They were at a draw,
neither one could move or gain any ground.
Bob asked Bob if he wanted to quit.
Bob was happy to oblige.
Bob went out the front door and puked,
and Bob went out the back door and puked.
They both went back in with more respect
for each other.
They both had another shot
of whiskey together.

Benedictions

When I climb into bed I lay on my back thinking awhile.
When I'm ready for black I roll onto my stomach,
palms up under my pillow.
It seems to prevent my arms and hands from becoming
dead hammers in the middle of the night.
When I have arranged myself comfortably I sometimes
mutter "thank you" aloud.
Not to anybody or anything.
Just for the fact that I'm snuggled down in my bed
and will quickly be asleep.
Tonight I followed this procedure,
but I shook myself awake to write this down.
Maybe I'll say "thank you" twice.

All Stopped Up

Driftwood clogging up the flow.
Backdraft blowing up her skirt,
fire down below.
Bridge caved in as soon as the
semi crossed.
Every time he blows smoke up
her ass, she keeps his buddies'
salad tossed.
Stamped his feet and broke
his jaw.
Jerked off in that woman's bra.
His face looked all caved in.
She rode his dead hard pecker
before she called it in.
Toe jam toe tag, body pushed
into the incinerator to burn.
Nothing left but ashes inside
 a shit-can urn.

Paving The Way

My stepdaughter Aidan and I have a waiting room
to ourselves.
All the other suckers are crowded in a small room
further down the hall.
We have pulled chairs together into makeshift cots
on opposite sides of a table.
We have slept and relaxed.
Aidan woke up once and polished off her chocolate
pudding and then fell back to sleep.
I have read, wrote, and gone to the pisser multiple
times.

My stepdaughter Lynna is in complete agony — an absolute
test of endurance in pain: mind, body, and spirit.
Sleep deprivation is weighing heavy on her as she is
working toward delivering her first child — my grandson.
She is fighting like she has never fought before.
All of the painful life experiences I have gone through
seem trivial to me right now.
I would easily take the pain to ease hers.
That's not an option.

Lynna is carving a brand new road.
What a goddamn glorious road it is.

Remedy

Sometimes there's no cure
for boredom except insanity.
A little slice of insanity
can do you up right.
I took a big piece and put
it through the blender.
Drank it down like a shake.
Then I beat the sides of my
head in with my fists.
Now I feel better.

Leftover

Joel polished the head of his pecker like a stone, and it
shined like a freshly waxed tile floor the night he
went out with her.
When he put on cologne, he also sprayed a liberal amount
on the underside of his cock and all over his balls.
It burned like hell, but he liked it because it made him feel
refreshed and alive.
Joel took Tiffany out to dinner and a movie in his Z28
Camaro, and her eyes and lungs were on fire from Joe's
Polo cologne.
She rolled her window partway down, but he told her to
roll it up — that he would crank the A/C.
Then she endured a freezing cold Camaro gas chamber.
The movie was a generic macho action flick — the kind
Tiffany detested.
Fifteen minutes in, Joel reached over and held her hand.
She thought it was strangely annoying when he began
kneading her hand like dough and, after awhile, it hurt.
Finding reasons to let go such as an itchy nose
or shifting into another position — his hand inevitably sought
hers out and captured it again

Dinner was the only thing that had been halfway decent. Joel picked an Italian restaurant she had never been to before.
Although the personal pan pizza had been very good, she was unable to eat it all, and the waiter boxed it up for her.
After the movie, Joel asked Tiffany what she wanted to do next?
She told him she needed to be getting on home because she was tired and had to be up early.
On the way he clammed up when she tried to make small talk.
He looked straight ahead and didn't say a word.
Arriving at her house, she opened the door and got out.
"I had a really nice time," she said picking up her leftovers, "it was a lot of fun."
"I'll take that," he said reaching out and nodding at the box in her hand.
"What?" she said.
He motioned with his fingers for her to place it in his hand.
Slowly she gave it to him, and he laid it in the passenger seat.
When she closed the door he rolled the window down.
"We should do it again sometime," he said.
Tiffany stood in disbelief as Joel casually drove away.

Beer Ticket

I pulled the pappy-in-law card because I wanted that Guinness ticket.
I couldn't stand it that he was going to give it to a stranger just because a stranger had given it to him.
I was just as needy as anyone else.
Even though we weren't flesh and blood, I figured we were close enough.
We had beer blood flowing through us that was thicker than water or anything else.

Charmer

He drifted along and tore his own head off.
Then he scaled along sucking up tidbits of shit through
his neck hole to sustain his infallible life
He had one of them ropey necks with veins
popping out when he was thinkin' hard or madder
than all get out.
It looked like a snake without a head to guide it.
He was snakelike too: cold and mean and lookin'
for the next angle to leave you flat as a flitter and
none the wiser until he'd slithered off in the deep
dark woods.
He had a way of springin' up when folks least
expected him to.

Low Pressure

It's a wandering system that's had its
umbilical cord cut from the jet stream.
It's slowly moving around pissing on
things.
Kinda like you and me.
We roam around occasionally pissing
on stuff.

Brother Angus

Angus, I'm killing your brother today.
Angus…There aren't no other way.
Angus, I'm sick of being slingshotted around the sun.
Angus, I'm killing your brother before the day is done.
Angus, hallelujah to you.
Angus, don't look so blue.
Angus, don't get crossways with me.
Angus, down on wounded knee.

Lucky Horseshoe

I'm drunk enough to sit in the rain and write this.
It feels good drinking.
It's "the water" of beers.
Olympia since 1896.
Not as good as 1897 when my grandma was born.
But… beer's got to be born too.
So I'm sure as hell not going to knock it.

Midway

She was the best looking girl at this hole-in-
the-wall bar on 29th Street in Choctaw.
She sang and swayed to the music.
All of a sudden the good ol' boy bartender
threw her out.
"Fuck you! You don't have a right!" she
yelled.
She got 86ed for running her mouth and
stealing peoples' drinks while they were
up using the bathroom, shooting pool, or
putting money in the jukebox.
What a shame.
She was the most interesting thing to
look at in here.

Up to the Rafters

Pack rat mind.
Dusty caverns filled with debris
that seems to go on for eternity.
Crammed to the gills with the past.
It germinates, festers, and bubbles
over with nowhere to go.

Drunken Dance Floor Girls

Twirling asses to the music.
Beautiful down-home butt shakin' around.
Boners aplenty.

The Meadow is Always Slipperier on the Other Side of the Fence

He was an old softy when it came to tight pussy.
He could never get enough.
If it were possible he would run knee-deep
in it.
He wouldn't wear waders or nothing.
It would make him happy to be sopping wet
with lamb pie.
One night he dreamt of a great big
field of cunts to frolic in.
It was a dream come true while it lasted.

Root Beer Fizz

Shitheels and shout-outs
Angry flies spinning about
Red mud on a dead man's boots
He came up missing after the turkey shoot
Pictures of Hollywood dames taped
to the bathroom stall
She screamed like a banshee
after the rooster's caw
He left Louisiana after they
whacked off his hand
He ended up in Oklahoma selling
whiskey disguised as a root beer stand

Saving it for Later

Default:
Declining days.
Digging dirt further
downward into
deprivation.
Earth worms tickling
privates.
Cream of the crop
wears tilting crown
of mud and Bermuda
roots.

Polishing The Empties

The snoring animals are
cutting logs next to half
drank cans of beer.
It's soothing.
I finish their beers.
Somebody's got to do it.
Might as well be me.

Sweet Breath

Early morning
Breathing
Lowering feet into shoes
Shoes hit the road
The road snakes like
a chaotic river
Juniper smoke rising in the air
The air thick with bees
The bees pollinate death
Death trickles in like honey

Seeing Will Squander Your Vision

Interest is falling through the roof of a house with no roof.
It leaves the people and their possessions wet, sticky, and smelling funky.
They don't entertain guests there, you can mark my words on that.
They trickle along under a sunbeam with shoes made out of lead.
Being crafty is the only way they get by at all.
The weasel has nothing on them.
They can make do with nothing more than an apricot pit.
You've gotta see it to believe it.

Rain Dance

The jet stream isn't blowing my way.
It's taking a big detour to leave me
high and dry.
High and dry.
Dry and high.
I hear that other places is getting
too much rain.
They should spread that shit out
and share with the rest of us.
Crops, trees, humans, and beasts
are dying in the dusty heat.
Let the clouds wage war with lightning
bolts and bombshell thunder above my head.
I want flash floods and creeks that are so
swollen that you have to give
them an anti-inflammatory.
Bring me cloudy days for days on end.
Nothing makes me happier than blotting
out the sun.
Looking out the window at a grey world
makes me ponder over things more.
But watching it rain really

strokes my brain cock.
So open up the sky dam and let the water
saturate the dry dead earth.
This is my plea.
This is my rain dance.

Laminated Heart on a Keychain

Glass dog pissing gasoline.
Sweet little honey eating up all the bees.
I keep on thinking, but horseshit
continues to pour out of my ears.
Kick the chins holding up the octopus.
Plant my ass a second.
Give my dogs a rest.

Obscured by Shit

Things have never been concrete, exactly.
They've never flourished in just one pot.
They have stewed, bubbled, and boiled over.
Gotten tired, moldy, and grew into something
alien or nothing at all.
All the pieces need to be at play.
Even then, deception's sticky fingers can prevent
a total conclusion.
It's a calamity when you keep digging deeper
and deeper.
When you don't just settle for the obvious facts.
Sometimes you can be left in total wonderment
at the confusion of it all.
Trust is a hard thing to gain when you're sloshing
around in bullshit.
The answers can be as clear as a freshly cleaned
piece of glass in the sunlight.
Or it can be like opening your eyes in a muddy
old cow pond.

Wintertide

I like winter.
I like how the trees show their bare bones to the world.
I like heavy coats, gloves, and stuffing my hands
in my pockets.
I like grey skies better than the sun.
I like long walks through the woods on cold cloudy days.
I like snow and how it completely changes the world.
I like opening all the curtains in my bedroom so I can
pause while I'm writing and see the beauty of the snow
covered trees.
The frigid temperatures make me crackle with energy
and open up wide vistas of creativity.
I like building big fires outside at night during
wintertime too.
Dragging up wood and keeping it cozy and warm
against the chill.
I like holding my girlfriend when we're around the
campfire.
I like walking through the woods in the snow on
mushrooms lit by the blue moon.
How every nook and every tree was lit up with an

uncanny brilliance.

All these things make me happy.

Winter, I hate to see you go.

Blood Cells and Barbed Wire

He walks on a straight razor,
and, like the snail, his protective coating
of slime prevents him from injury.
He once said: "If lightning ever strikes me
for my sins, it'll only energize me
and make me stronger."
Then he shouted at the clear blue sky,
"Come on god, you stupid motherfucker, strike
me with a lightning bolt so I can fuck all day
like the Energizer bunny!"
He lived on a diet of crawdads and prune juice.
He drank moonshine from an old saucer that
depicted Popeye squeezing a can of spinach into
his mouth on the rare occasions that he scored
it for free.
He was the kind of man that made everyone
nervous when he entered the room.
He was small, but he had epileptic
horses bucking in his eyes.
One day he was banned from the local café for
jumping table to table and preaching his

politics that nobody understood.
It had to do with blood cells and barbwire and
how everyone was linked through cockroach wings.
He rode a bicycle that he built from parts he found
at the dump, and he claimed it was the fastest
bicycle on earth, as well as a couple of other
planets nobody had ever heard of.

Where Angels Go to Hell

There wasn't anything else to do.
All the fun stuff had run its course and where
ideas used to be spring fed was now a dried up
creek bed.
It's within these barren times that bad ideas
get brewed.
A person might cut his own hand just to feel
something, anything, to make sure they were still alive.
It was during this period that a lot of fights,
stabbings, and shootings occurred.
It got to be such a regular thing that it wasn't
much different than somebody drinking a
cup of coffee in the morning.
There were three or four funerals daily,
and once it tallied up to nine.
The people were out of tears, and men and women
alike would stand at the gravesides like blackened
weeds, staring through red-rimmed eyes into
a desolate void that held no future.
People started staying at home to avoid trouble,
but sometimes trouble would come to them when

trouble was bored and didn't have anything else to do.
The sheriff moved away early on when he saw
a noose in a tree with his name on it.
There was no protection and everyone fended
for themselves.
Like ostracized wolves they roamed alone.
Nobody wanted to leave but no one knew why.
They kept waking up, doing their chores, burying
the dead, and staring at the wall.
There was nowhere else for them.
They had created this place.
Now the place owned them.

A Line in the Dirt

Lines are drawn and blood is spilled.
Vultures and gore cover the landscape.
Men could be seen sitting in pools of their comrades'
blood staring motionless like ghosts of battle.
They did not answer when spoken to
and did not flinch when struck across the face.
These are the victors.
They are hard men, and combat and bloodshed
is all they have known in life.
All they cared about.
Nobody knew what they'd seen but it was
something other than the onslaught.
The comatose men have taken part in many atrocities
far, far worse than this.
It was noted by some that quite a few bodies on
the battlefield hadn't been slain by a sword.
They had been torn apart by something much
more sinister.
A savage animal they agreed, but no beast
that they knew of could tear someone
apart like this.

The torpid men would not cooperate as they
tried in vain to get them to their feet.
After a day of trials and discussion, the decision
was made to leave them behind.
There were too many of them to take by force,
and it was too far of a journey home.
Their greatest warriors were left behind to die
of dehydration, to be eaten by carrion birds.
As living men they were dead to this world.

Original

He thought he was a man of profound words,
but he was a liar.
He thought he was a man of consequence,
but he was a drippy dick
driveling into a toilet sea.
He thought he had it all figured out,
but he had drawn his map with a turd.
He thought he had a right to criticize others,
but he was just another jack-off
who hung out in coffee shops and poetry readings.
He thought he was out to save the world,
but I would rather spend an eternity in
flames than live in the one he has in mind.
He thought he was part of a new Beat generation,
but the only thing he beats
is his worthless little pecker.
He is all you sorry bastards
that can't come up with anything original.

Norman Nights

Swirling city streets,
lights go by in sheets and streaks.
The steering wheel never felt
so out of place in my hands.
Grazed a bright orange construction barrel.
I drive on.
Have to get off the main street:
    confused,
      dizzy,
        nauseous —
going to get sick.
The car hugs the side street as best as it can
with a flipped out, tripping drunkard
puking out the door.
Can't find my friend's house,
no sense of direction.
No sense at all.
Somehow find my way back to the bar,
missed the drive, can't turn around.
Goddamn construction.
This is it,

swing the car next right,
parallel park.
Not too bad for a fuck up.

Special thanks to Ryan Lawson
for his help in editing these poems.

The following poems were originally published by
Electric Chair Press:

Well-Done

Peckerhead Jones

Tension

Good Morning America

Silt

Getting It

Mother Nature

Discovery

Bean Dip

Winnie the Pooh and Tiger Too

The Big Squeeze

Fire Water

Piss Pants

Turning On the Dead

Common Swarm

Out Cold

Pumice

Silted In

Chicken Killer

Burn Pile

Skin

R.J.

Puking Bobs

Obscured By Shit

Original

Norman Nights

Photo by Marissa Johnson

ABOUT THE AUTHOR:

Robert Spencer lives in Choctaw, Oklahoma.

Made in the USA
Charleston, SC
05 February 2016